# NEW MEXICO'S
## PUEBLO
## BASEBALL LEAGUE

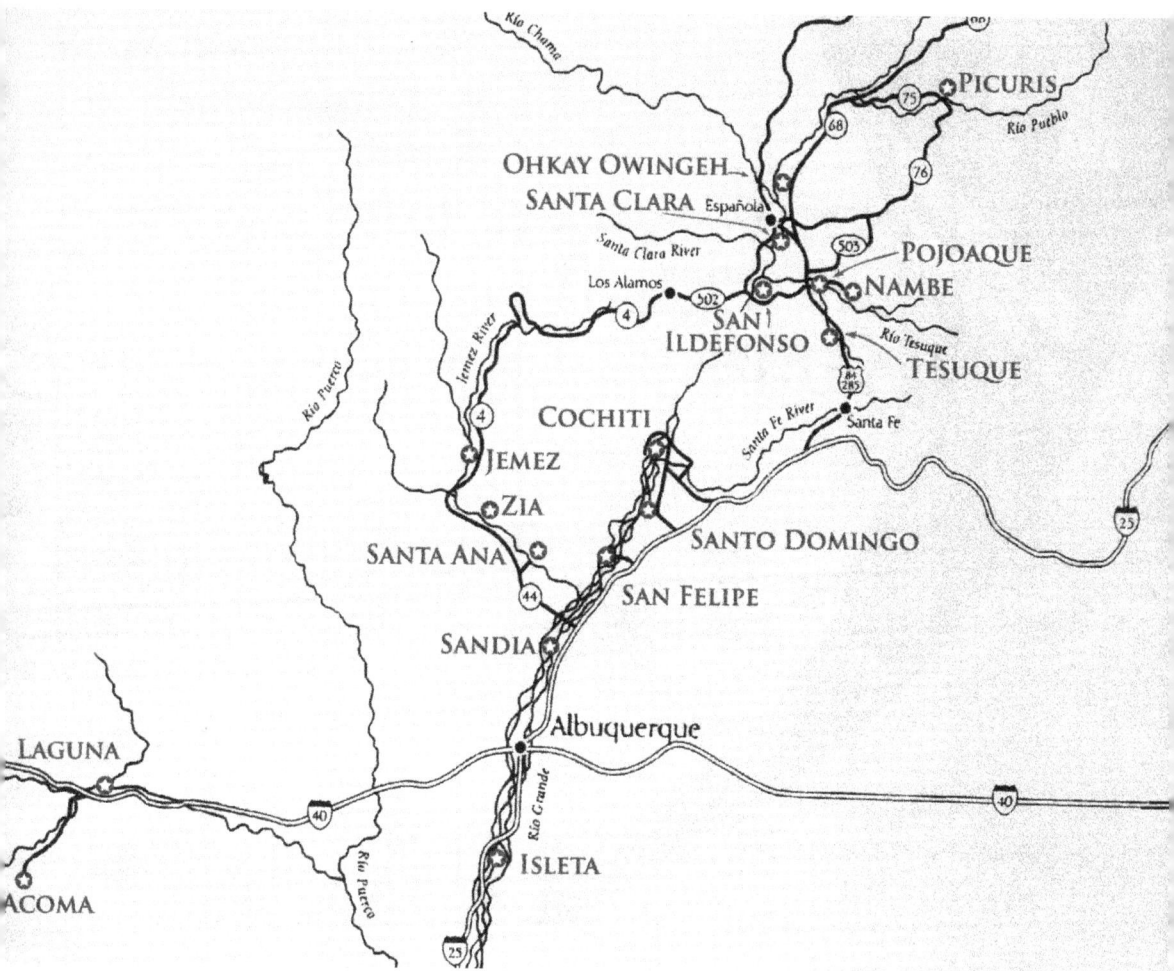

There are 19 pueblos in New Mexico located along the Rio Grande, its tributaries, and other rivers. The two pueblos not shown on this map are Zia (beyond the border to the lower left) and Taos (beyond the border in the upper right). It does include the "historical" baseball pueblos, such as Isleta, Laguna, Tesuque, Cochiti, and Ohkay Owingeh. (Courtesy of Indian Pueblo Cultural Center, Albuquerque.)

**FRONT COVER:** This c. 1930 photograph is titled "Playing Baseball at Tesuque Pueblo." (Courtesy of Palace of the Governors Photo Archives.)

**COVER BACKGROUND:** The Pueblos are playing the Navajos in the 2007 Pueblo/Navajo All-Star Game. (Courtesy of Randy Sinner.)

**BACK COVER:** A young boy watches and learns baseball at Santa Ana Pueblo while sitting next to a relative. (Photograph by Herb Howell.)

# NEW MEXICO'S PUEBLO BASEBALL LEAGUE

*James D. Baker, Herbert Howell, and Marie A. Cordero*

ARCADIA
PUBLISHING

Copyright © 2015 by James D. Baker, Herbert Howell, and Marie A. Cordero
ISBN 978-1-5316-7728-2

Published by Arcadia Publishing
Charleston, South Carolina

Library of Congress Control Number: 2014954331

For all general information, please contact Arcadia Publishing:
Telephone 843-853-2070
Fax 843-853-0044
E-mail sales@arcadiapublishing.com
For customer service and orders:
Toll-Free 1-888-313-2665

Visit us on the Internet at www.arcadiapublishing.com

JDB: *For my late wife Madalyn Baker*
HH: *For my daughter Autumn Howell*
MAC: *For my uncle Joseph C. Quintana*

# CONTENTS

# ACKNOWLEDGMENTS

The authors wish to give special thanks to the following for their contributions to the information, images, and publication of this book: Hanna Abelbeck, Jimmy Abeita, Sam Arquero, Stacia Bannerman, Rosa Diaz, Domenic Gachupin, Anne Gonzales, Jay Herrera, Rob Kangas, Ray Leon, Terry Leon, Joyce Leon-Sanders, Dottie Lopez, Larry Phillips, Joseph C. Quintana, Patrick Reardon, Grace Roybal, Robert Shendo, Joseph Suina, and David Wheelock.

# FOREWORD

My buddy and I never went anywhere, it seems, without a fly ball arching across the sky between us as we walked a couple hundred feet apart. We would throw the ball as high as a nine-year-old's strength would allow, testing the fielding ability of the boy on the receiving end. We alternated between lobbing fly balls and skipping grounders at top speed, sometimes off to the side, to make it more challenging. The fielder would try to scoop up a grounder like a hotshot shortstop and fire it back in one seamless motion, imagining throwing out a runner inches before scoring the winning run. We practiced fielding, hitting, running, and even sliding in this way, outside the context of an organized game. And, of course, we played the game any time there were enough players around. We included girls when we had to. Our obsession with the game of baseball was clearly a reflection of the adult preoccupation with the game in the village.

Our dads and uncles spoke often about Cochiti baseball from a time beyond my memory. They played with non-Indians from surrounding Hispanic villages and from the white mining towns toward the east mountain areas. Madrid and Cerrillos, still thriving communities into the 1940s, had men always eager to play ball against the Pueblo Indians from the Rio Grande area. Outside of tourists, baseball brought the greatest early acquaintance with the white community for my dad's generation. From what I understand, the league was not as well organized and regular as the later Indian leagues I became familiar with. But, by far, the most remembered games were those they played inside the New Mexico State Penitentiary in Santa Fe. Needless to say, they did not have any Pueblo home games with those guys. Listening to the descriptions of the prison environment and about the one or two men "on the inside" who were professional-caliber players, I could tell that our predecessors were enthralled by their experiences. One giant African American man pitched a fiery fastball where, as one player put it, "we couldn't see the ball but swung at it anyway, well after the ball had hit the catcher's mitt." Our relatives would laugh and recall lots of details of prisoners, fascinating those of us who were not present for the events. This was in keeping with the mode of storytelling still central in our Native life.

By the time I understood the finer points of the game, we could count on a baseball game on any summer Sunday afternoon in the pueblo. The game engaged the young and the old in our village in the same way it did in almost all the pueblos in New Mexico. Each participating village had at least two adult male teams that played for either the South or the North Pueblo League. In addition, there was the Santa Fe Jays. The lone team made up of urban Indians, it later began recruiting players from the Pueblo reservations. The recruits were for the most part good players discontented with the amount of playing time they were receiving back home. The two Indian leagues had enough teams and interest to play a game each week in the pueblo from early May to early September.

The two teams from our village were fierce rivals, and the two regular-season games we played against each other were always heated, with hecklers adding to the emotion of the contests. Otherwise, one team from the village played at home on any given week while the other was away. On game day, the visiting team from another pueblo rode into town, fans in tow hungry for a victory. Hollering and honking horns after a hit or a run broke the silence of a lazy summer afternoon in the village area. Taunting the opposition was a fan specialty that, on occasion, turned personal and ended up in hurt feelings that went beyond the diamond. From time to time, a drunken fan or a player brought emotions to a boil, and the benches would empty very quickly. After a victory, parading vehicles honking through the village woke up sleeping dogs and a few residents who would rather nap on a lazy afternoon.

Each pueblo had two baseball fields at the edge of the community where all the action took place. The fields were pieced together with materials found or acquired with little or no monetary expenditure. This was long before grant money or other funding sources for recreational programs could build facilities for communities. Half a dozen tall posts stood several yards behind home plate, supporting the stretch of chicken wire that served as the backstop. The bases were discards from city teams, who gave them to the Indians as an act of charity. The team dugouts were made from scrap lumber—just enough to provide shade for the players and to store the equipment outside the playing field. Our fields did not have outfield fences for home runs to fly over. The outfielders paced from side to side, waiting for the ball to drop into the area where the ball field opened up to the sagebrush, cactus, and yucca plants. Bleachers were unheard of; fans sat under umbrellas along the sidelines next to the team they were rooting for or behind the backstop to catch a glimpse of what the pitcher had to deliver. Some sat on the tailgates of pickup trucks backed in along the sideline, facing away from the field to safeguard windshields from foul balls.

And, speaking of foul balls, they had to be shagged immediately, since we had only two or three new game balls to play with. If a batter hit three foul balls in succession, the game came to a halt until a ball came back in. The rest of the equipment was an assortment of hand-me-downs acquired from who knows where. Most of the bats were cracked and heavily taped at the grip. Many gloves, and even some shoe spikes, were held together with tape as well. Some players had full uniforms, and others lacked a shirt or pants, replaced with blue jeans and a sweatshirt. Nothing matched, but there was still a lot of team pride and loyalty.

For away games, team members and their fans gathered by the village store if they needed a ride. A pickup truck would come by and load up until it was full. Players always had priority. If there was not enough room for everyone in a vehicle, some fans would have to wait for another one, which would come by shortly. Almost everyone who wanted to go to the game got to go. There was always a stop in a nearby town before reaching our destination, where adults pitched in to get a loaf of bread and bologna for lunch and some Cokes for all to share. Lunch was for everyone who traveled; who paid and who did not was never an issue.

Once in a great while, there were not enough players to field a team due to some unexpected circumstance. Perhaps a vehicle broke down, or the game conflicted with an event back home. In such a situation, the team with less than nine players would forfeit and chalk up a loss, a drastic outcome at season's end when a team's won-loss record determined if it would get into the playoffs. One Sunday, I piled into a truck with a couple of the players, old man John Velasquez, and some ladies and their children and headed for a game at Santa Clara Pueblo, some 50 miles away. When we got there, it was nearly 2:00 p.m., the scheduled game time. Our team was shy one player, and the manager kept looking anxiously down the road, hoping that another vehicle would bring the much-needed player. The home team was on the field, hoping just the opposite. Our team, the Cochiti Braves, was one of the top teams in the league, and our opponents were eager to have us lose without having to play us. With just five minutes left, Silviano, the manager, carrying a spare team shirt, hurried to where John and I were sitting. I was 13 years old, considered too young to play according to some unspoken rule. So, it was John that Silviano tried to encourage to fill in until someone showed up. John responded that he could not run and used every possible ache and pain to weasel out of playing. At the last minute, the frustrated manager threw the spare baseball shirt at me and ordered me out to the dugout, where my name was added to the lineup without a chance for me to protest. After our first three outs, I found myself in right field, wearing a Braves baseball shirt, a glove in my hand, and the oversized manager's cap on my head. I struck out easily my first time at bat. The next time up, the pitcher, thinking I was an easy out, threw me an easy ball. I stepped into it with my best swing and hit a double! My third time up, he hit me, and I took my base. I managed another hit on the day and scored a couple of times. I was credited, at the very least, for the team not forfeiting; but, more important, we won the game. That began my career in Pueblo Indian League baseball, for which I played regularly at third base for the next four years before I left for the Marine Corps after high school. I also played that position throughout my Bernalillo High School years. On that team, seven of the starters were from Cochiti.

Sunday games continued through the long, hot summer season. The only interruption occurred on the Fourth of July, when the best players competed in the all-star game between the North and South Leagues. I was fortunate enough to play four times as the third baseman for the North League. Each position had two players selected for this prestigious game. At stake were not just bragging rights and individual recognition; these all-star games were attended by huge crowds drawn from throughout Pueblo country.

No one from Cochiti in this era went on to play baseball in college, as far as I know. Very few Indians went to college then, and there was no opportunity for exposure to professional play. We did hear that some of our players excelled on teams while serving in the military, including what would amount to battalion intramural teams, as was my experience at Camp Pendleton. But kids from many pueblos did play big parts on high school championship teams.

The game was loved by our predecessors, just as we loved it. You can still hear honking horns and hollering fans any summer Sunday afternoon here today, and I am sure those sounds will be made by our children and by those yet to be born.

—Joseph Suina, PhD
Governor, Cochiti Pueblo, 2014

# INTRODUCTION

"Born to play baseball." This is said often about Native Americans in New Mexico, and it is what many Native Americans believe. They play with pride, intensity, competitiveness, and skill. Players match a strong love of the game with uncanny natural ability. Because of these combined characteristics, there is no ethnic group in the United States that exceeds the Native Americans. The Pueblos in New Mexico have been playing baseball for over 115 years. As a result, the sport has become an integral part of Pueblo life and culture. This book offers a photographic story of their adventures.

One of the challenges in the creation of this book was the lack of photographic images. Photography, in addition to sketching and recording, are not generally allowed in the pueblos, which results in few available images. Those that do exist are sometimes hard to locate. And, when some are found, acquiring permission for their use can be difficult. Also, very few baseball records were kept. Early games and players were occasionally described in newspaper articles, but this was an exception.

The photographs presented here come from various sources. Many were contributed by Pueblo members and have not been seen outside the Native American community. Others have been found in archives throughout the country. And some images are from the authors, who took photographs with permission of the Pueblos. Together, the images that follow represent a story that has not been told before.

The book is organized into sections covering the following topics: the 2014 season opener, which presents a contemporary game and environment; the origins of Native American baseball in New Mexico, which also appears to be the origins of Native American baseball in North America; the Indian schools, where many Pueblos and other Native Americans learned to play baseball; the organization and evolution of the league; some of the historic baseball pueblos; the 2007 all-star game between the best of the Pueblos and the best of the Navajos; and, finally, a look at baseball at the Cochiti Pueblo, especially the Cochiti Braves, covering a span of over 80 years.

10

# 1

# OPENING DAY 2014

The arrival of Mother's Day each year signals the beginning of the Pueblo Baseball League season in New Mexico. On this day, and on most Saturdays and Sundays until Labor Day, teams take the field to play each other in either the North or South divisions of the league.

Bad weather is seldom a factor. It may be raining, the sand may be blowing, or the temperature may be over 100 degrees, but unless the field is flooded, the game will go on.

The players, donning their respective uniforms (which they must wear), range from 17 to 55 years of age. Young, very strong, athletic men play alongside older, not-so-athletic men. Some of the young players have college baseball experience, and a few have been invited to try out for professional teams.

The games are almost always played on a barren, dusty field. There are some metal stands, but many of the spectators remain in their automobiles, which are parked around the field. The players come to the game already dressed, or they dress in the parking lot in cars or vans.

While the game itself is serious, the environment is festive. Friends and family from both pueblos are there to support their team. There is a "tailgating" atmosphere, and children play their own games just beyond the diamond.

The game presented in this chapter is iconic in the sense that the images represent many of the ideas illustrated in this book. The teams are the Cochiti Braves and the Jemez Hawks.

It is the opening day of the Pueblo Baseball League. This game, between the Jemez Hawks and the Cochiti Braves, is being played at Braves Field, located at Cochiti Pueblo, New Mexico.

(Photograph by James Baker.)

Braves pitcher Jared Quintana is starting his windup. A Hawks player takes a lead from first base. (Photograph by James Baker.)

A Hawks pitcher begins his throw as a Braves player attempts to steal second base. (Photograph by James Baker.)

Braves players and children mingle in front of the dugout. It is common for children to be allowed in this area while the game is in progress. (Photograph by James Baker.)

Hawks players monitor the action in their dugout during the game. (Photograph by James Baker.)

While there are three sets of metal stands, spectators often prefer to sit in their automobiles surrounding the field. The above photograph shows automobiles parked between home plate and first base. Below, spectators and their cars are shown beyond the outfield. (Both photographs by James Baker.)

The games are festive events. Many friends and family treat it as a tailgating opportunity. (Photograph by James Baker.)

The concession stand offers numerous items and refreshments to spectators. Admission to the game is free, so this is a source of revenue for the Braves team. (Photograph by James Baker.)

Animals are often present at the games. The dog shown above seems unimpressed with the proceedings. Below, horses sometimes respond to cheers from the spectators. Also, wild horses roam the mountains in this area. Three of them raced across the field during a later season game. (Both photographs by James Baker.)

The game is truly a family affair. Children form and play their own games just beyond the playing field. (Both photographs by James Baker.)

As mentioned on page 11, games in the Pueblo Baseball League are rarely called because of weather. In this case, a sandstorm blew in—but the game continued. (Both photographs by James Baker.)

# 2

# THE ORIGIN OF
# PUEBLO BASEBALL

The earliest documented instance of Native American baseball in North America is in 1863 according to the book *Games of the North American Indians* by Stewart Culin. The book resulted from several studies of Native American games around 1900. The narrative recounts that the Navajos learned baseball from soldiers while imprisoned at Basque Redondo near Fort Sumner, New Mexico. The Navajos' imprisonment lasted from 1863 to 1866.

The early game was somewhat different than it is today. One variation is that the bases were run in a clockwise direction. Also, a runner could be tagged by a person with the ball or be hit by a thrown ball. The runner could go to any length to avoid being tagged or hit.

A number of different games were played by Native Americans before the introduction of baseball, one of the most popular being "shinny." This was very much like the sport of field hockey as played today. Sticks were carved by the players; the ball was made of animal skin and could be filled with cotton. Shinny was played by both males and females, and by males and females together. The playing field varied in length, but it could be up to two miles long. There was competition among the pueblos, which could be serious and intense. Often, the losing pueblo would have to provide a service to the winners, such as cleaning storm drains.

Other games included "hoop and pole," in which a ring was tossed into the air and players competed to catch it with their pole or spear.

The last part of this chapter includes photographs of pueblos at the time baseball was beginning in the area. The images, taken between 1880 and 1920, are intended to illustrate what pueblo life was like at the time.

# New Mexico

Basque
Redondo

(Fort Sumner)

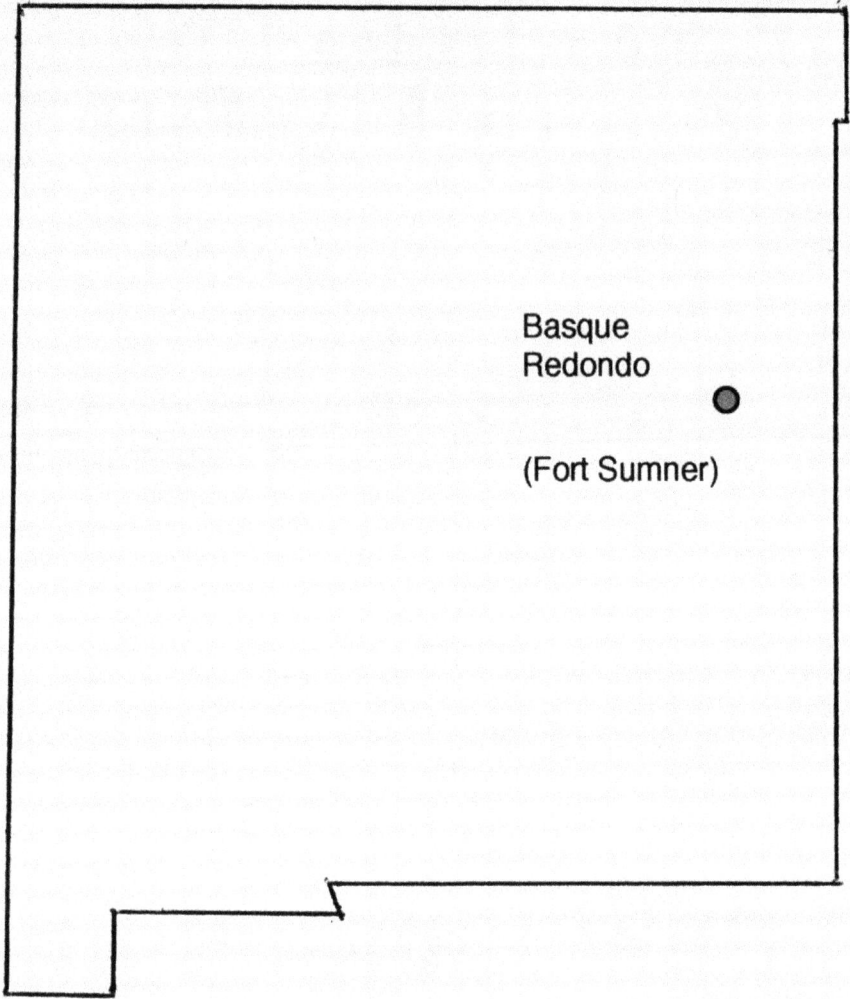

Basque Redondo was where the Navajos were imprisoned and is near Fort Sumner, located in east central New Mexico. (Courtesy of James Baker.)

These photographs depict Navajos at Basque Redondo. The conditions were extremely difficult, including drastic variations in cold and hot weather, as well as inadequate food and water. There was considerable suffering and death during this period. Above, Navajos are being guarded by soldiers between 1863 and 1868. The photograph below, dated 1866, is a street view of Fort Sumner. (Both courtesy of the Palace of the Governors Photo Archives; above 028534, below 028539.)

A memorial has been constructed at Basque Redondo to honor the suffering of the Navajos during their imprisonment there. (Photograph by Grace Roybal.)

THE ORIGIN OF PUEBLO BASEBALL

Shinny, which predates baseball, was a game played by most indigenous peoples in North America. It was similar to today's sport of field hockey. Early photographs of Native Americans playing shinny are extremely rare. This painting, by Oscar Howe, depicts a shinny game. (Courtesy of South Dakota Historical Society.)

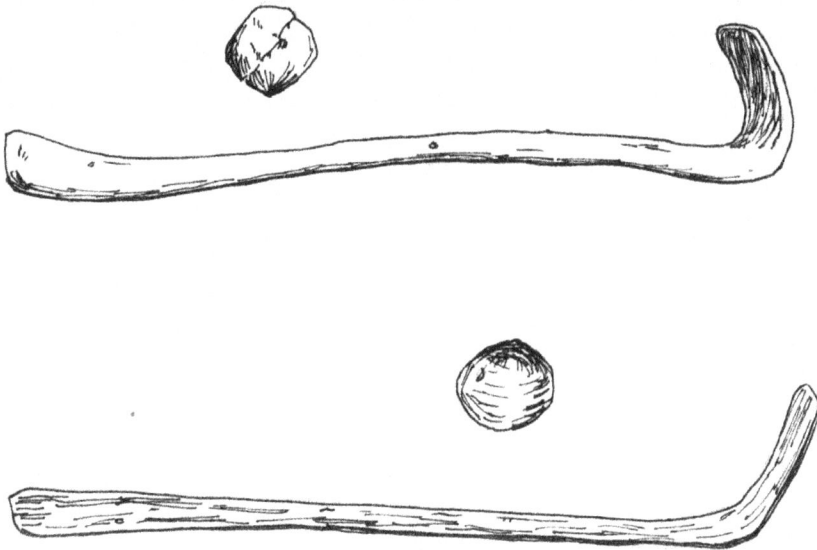

This is a drawing of shinny sticks and balls. The sticks, carved from wood by the players, are approximately 40 inches in length. The balls are about four inches in diameter and are made of animal skins, usually deerskin, and are stuffed with cotton. (Drawing by Lane Baker.)

This is a very rare photograph of Native Americans playing shinny. The game is being held in a plaza area in front of the church at Isleta Pueblo. The date is uncertain, but it is thought to be before 1900. Note the shinny sticks in the left center that the boys are using. (Courtesy of Valentino Jaramillo.)

Another painting by Oscar Howe illustrates the game of hoop and pole, which was also played before baseball. A ring (hoop) is tossed into the air, and the participants attempt to catch it with their poles. (Courtesy of South Dakota Historical Society.)

Early Native Americans played many ball games. Here, Acoma Indians play an unknown ball game near Enchanted Mesa in a 1920 photograph. (Courtesy of Palace of the Governors Photo Archives, 041600.)

NEW MEXICO'S PUEBLO BASEBALL LEAGUE

This photograph, and the four that follow, illustrate the environment of the pueblos at the time baseball began to be played in the region. Shown here in 1925 is Santa Ana Pueblo. (Courtesy of Palace of the Governors Photo Archives, 004096.)

THE ORIGIN OF PUEBLO BASEBALL

This is another view of Santa Ana Pueblo. The date of the photograph is unknown. (Courtesy of Palace of the Governors Photo Archives, 042707.)

This image of Ohkay Owingeh Pueblo (San Juan) was taken from the main plaza looking west. The date is believed to be 1912. (Courtesy of Palace of the Governors Photo Archives, 042408.)

In Ohkay Owingeh Pueblo, a group of Tewa women and children are seen in front of a house sometime between 1915 and 1920. (Courtesy of Palace of the Governors Photo Archives, 043064.)

This photograph, taken by T. Harmon Purkurst, shows Tesuque Pueblo. It is dated between 1915 and 1920. (Courtesy of Palace of the Governors Photo Archives, 012523.)

# 3

# INDIAN SCHOOLS

Baseball was taking hold in the pueblos by 1900. At this point, the first team composed entirely of Native Americans was formed at Isleta. It is not known exactly how baseball expanded from humble beginnings with the Navajos in 1863 to become a major Pueblo activity between 1900 and 1920. There are almost no written records of the sport, and there are few first- and second-generation Native American players alive to provide stories of the past. In addition, interviews that have been conducted often provide inconsistent accounts. It is almost certain that the game was learned from multiple sources. There is some documentation indicating that baseball was learned by Native American students while they were being boarded in the Indian schools.

The goals of the Indian schools were to Americanize Native Americans and accelerate their integration into the dominant culture. The students' participation in this was not voluntary. They were taken from their tribes and shipped to a school somewhere in the country. For most, the Indian school experience was not positive. Students were forced to wear their clothes and hair in the Anglo American style, and they were not schooled in their native languages. For some, however, the experience was not completely negative. There are those that credit the Indian schools with their later success.

The most famous of these schools was Carlisle Indian Industrial School in Pennsylvania. It was started in 1879 and became the model for some 200 such schools sponsored by the government and located throughout the country. Other schools included Hastings in Kansas and Riverside in Oklahoma.

There were three Indian schools in New Mexico. Albuquerque Indian School was founded in the 1880s, the Santa Fe Indian School in 1890, and St. Catherine's in Santa Fe in 1894. The Santa Fe Indian School is the only Indian school in the country still in existence. It is operated by the 19 New Mexico pueblos.

Carlisle in Pennsylvania was the first and most famous of the Indian schools. The student body was composed of Native Americans from throughout the United States. Some students excelled as athletes, such as Jim Thorpe. This 1900 photograph, taken by Maynard Hoover, shows the class of that year. The students have been divided into male and female sections. (Courtesy of Cumberland County Historical Society.)

Shown here is a group of Navajos from New Mexico at Carlisle. John N. Choate took this photograph around 1880. (Courtesy of Palace of the Governors Photo Archives, 087562.)

INDIAN SCHOOLS

Pueblo Indian students from New Mexico are shown at Carlisle around 1880. The photograph was taken by John N. Choate. (Courtesy of Palace of the Governors Photo Archives, 089078.)

An early Carlisle baseball team is shown in this c. 1891 photograph. The man in the center is Fisk Goodyear, who was associated with Glen "Pop" Warner for many years in the athletics of Native American students. (Courtesy of Cumberland County Historical Society, PA-CH2-025.)

Sometime between 1895 and 1900, C.G. Kaadt took this photograph of the US government Indian school in Santa Fe. The buildings shown here are, from left to right, the hospital, employees' home, girls' building, boys' building, and the school building. (Courtesy of Palace of the Governors Photo Archives, 001391.)

Pictured is the 1953 Santa Fe Indian School baseball team. The photographer was Harold Henson. (Courtesy of Palace of the Governors Photo Archives, HP.2009.90.32.)

St. Catherine's Industrial Indian
School has been closed for
many years. To date, attempts
to use the building and land
have not been successful. Boards
cover several of the windows.
(Photograph by James Baker.)

Tyler Dingee took this
c. 1950 photograph of
boys playing marbles at
St. Catherine's Industrial
Indian School. (Courtesy
of Palace of the Governors
Photo Archives, 120253.)

Here, girls play softball at St. Catherine's. A nun is observing the activity in the background. Tyler Dingee took this photograph around 1950. (Courtesy of Palace of the Governors Photo Archives, 120247.)

INDIAN SCHOOLS

The first Indian school in New Mexico was located in Albuquerque. It was established in the 1880s and had a church affiliation. This photograph, by J.R. Riddle, was taken about 1886. (Courtesy of Palace of the Governors Photo Archives, 076062.)

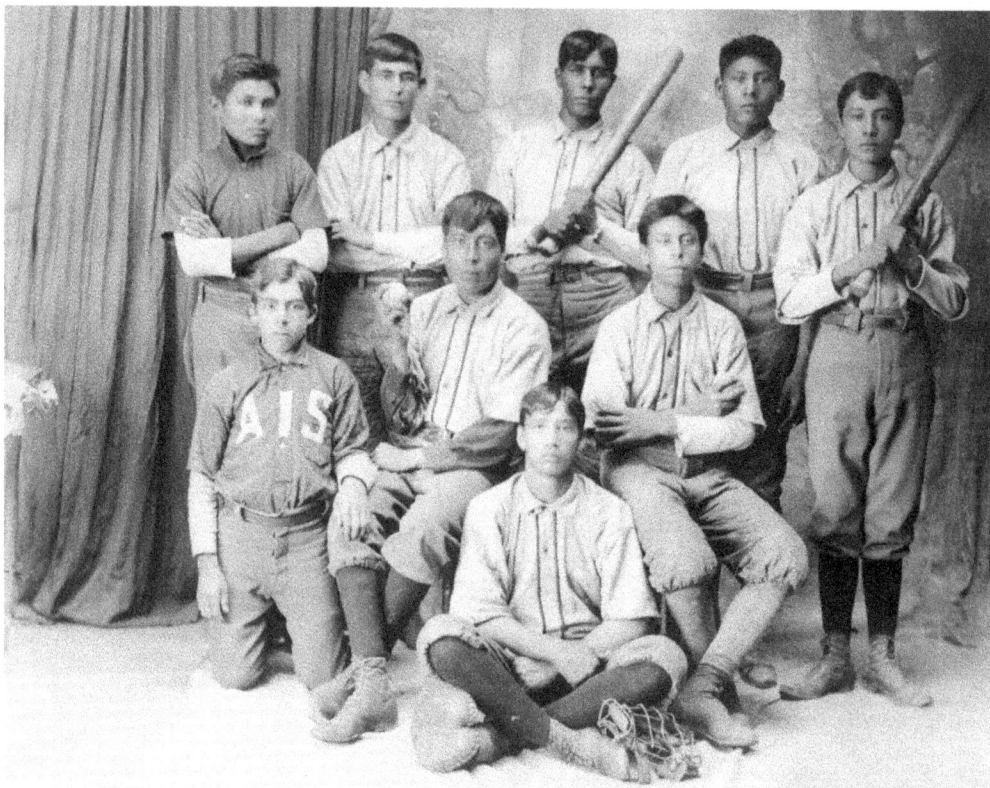

Above, the Albuquerque Indian School baseball team poses in 1900. This was about the same time as the beginning of a Pueblo Indian team at nearby Isleta Pueblo. The Albuquerque Indian School attracted Native Americans from throughout the Southwest, as well as from area pueblos. Newspaper archives fail to include any record of this school's games until around 1935, when it played Saint Mary's Academy of Albuquerque. Some players from Albuquerque Indian School returned to the pueblos after World War II and began playing baseball informally or in the Albuquerque City League. (Above, courtesy of Southwestern Archives, Zimmerman Library, University of New Mexico; below, Palace of the Governors Photo Archives.)

Albuquerque Indian School players pose in front of a 1949 Ford coupe (far right) in 1950. Pitcher Andy Leon (right) wears a Santa Ana Cubs jersey. The school played a variety of local teams, including men's adult teams, in the early years. It also competed against local high school teams. (Courtesy of the Leon family of Tamaya.)

Players on the Albuquerque Indian School team pose in their team jerseys in 1950. A few of these players appear in team pictures from other pueblos. Pitcher Andy Leon is in the second row, second from the right. (Courtesy of the Leon family.)

Manuel G. Saenz (first row, center) was originally from Isleta Pueblo. He was educated at the Haskell Institute (Indian school) in Kansas. He became a boys' advisor at Fort Totten. After that, Saenz was an advisor at other Bureau of Indian Affairs schools in Arizona and New Mexico, including Santa Fe from 1915 to 1926. (Courtesy of Palace of the Governors Photo Archives.)

# 4

# THE LEAGUE

The first all-Pueblo team was believed to be at Isleta around 1900. The end of the current Pueblo Baseball League season will mark 115 years of all-Pueblo baseball teams. Competition among Pueblo teams began in 1935 with the tournament at Laguna, which was also the site of the first league with teams only from the pueblo. The league as it is today began in 1960. There are two divisions, comprising teams from pueblos in the north and those in the south. Santa Fe is the approximate north/south divide, with Cochiti having played in the North League at some point. The championship game between the north and south pueblos began around 1960. The North/ South All-Star Game began shortly after that. The first all-star game between the Pueblos and Navajos was in 2002.

The Pueblo Baseball League has an extremely informal organization. The rules, though rarely set down in written form, are enforced by the pueblos. Today, the league has adopted the rules of the National League of Major League Baseball. Prior to this, the last time written rules were set down was about 15 years ago.

An important part of the league is the umpires. Baseball games have prescribed structures, rules, and guidelines for playing and officiating. Since the beginning, the role of the umpire has been an esteemed and demanding one. Whether popular or not, the umpire is charged with neutrality in the enforcement of the rules of the game. Some consider the umpire to be "baseball's policeman."

In New Mexico's Pueblo baseball system, the home team provides the home-plate umpire, and the visiting team usually provides the base umpire. Some umpires are well trained, while others are casual participants or last-minute volunteers from the bleachers. An unusual aspect of the league's umpiring is in regard to field responsibilities. In Pueblo baseball, the plate umpire also covers third base, while the other umpire covers only first and second bases. There is no true rotation of responsibilities. Additionally, an umpire works the entire season for just one team except in the playoffs.

# Pueblo Baseball Development

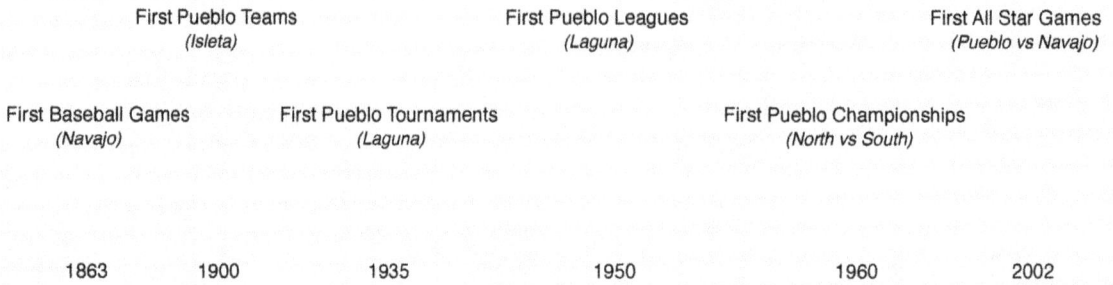

| | | | | | |
|---|---|---|---|---|---|
| | First Pueblo Teams *(Isleta)* | | First Pueblo Leagues *(Laguna)* | | First All Star Games *(Pueblo vs Navajo)* |
| First Baseball Games *(Navajo)* | | First Pueblo Tournaments *(Laguna)* | | First Pueblo Championships *(North vs South)* | |
| 1863 | 1900 | 1935 | 1950 | 1960 | 2002 |

This chart displays the progression of the New Mexico Pueblo baseball leagues. Key events mark the development of the Pueblo baseball leagues, leading to the present day. (Courtesy of James Baker and Herb Howell.)

# CONSTITUTION OF THE SOUTHERN INDIAN BASEBALL LEAGUE

## ARTICLE I

This organization shall be known as the Southern Indian Baseball League, playing under the rules of the National Baseball Congress of America.

The purpose of the organization shall be to promote, govern and conduct nonprofessional baseball in the Southern Division of Indian Baseball.

## ARTICLE II

## LEAGUE OFFICIALS

### SECTION 1:

In the Southern Division Baseball League, there shall be a President, Vice-President, and Secretary- Treasurer. The Officers of the League shall act as the Organization's Executive Committee. These Officers shall be elected by the Managers every two (2) terms or hold duly elected. No officers may serve more than two (2) terms or hold more than one (1) office at a time.

### SECTION 2:

Each team manager may designate one (1) individual who shall serve as the team's official representative and spokesman at all League meetings. If the manager of official team representative is not able to be present at the League meeting, they shall instruct the Secretary of its Division as to which individual will serve in his stead at the meeting.

### SECTION 3:

The Official team representative and the elected officers of the League shall be the Executive Council of the Divisional League ( see Section 1).

### SECTION 4:

The Executive Committee may be terminated as follows:

A. By resignation
B. By act of the Council
C. By reaching the term required

A section of the constitution of the South Pueblo League is shown here. Most of these rules, dating to the turn of the 20th century, are still in place today. In 2013, the South League adopted Major League Baseball's National League rules as its standard. This called for the use of wooden bats instead of metal bats, the removal of the designated hitter, and the dropping of the sanctions against pitchers when hitting batters. (Courtesy of Herb Howell.)

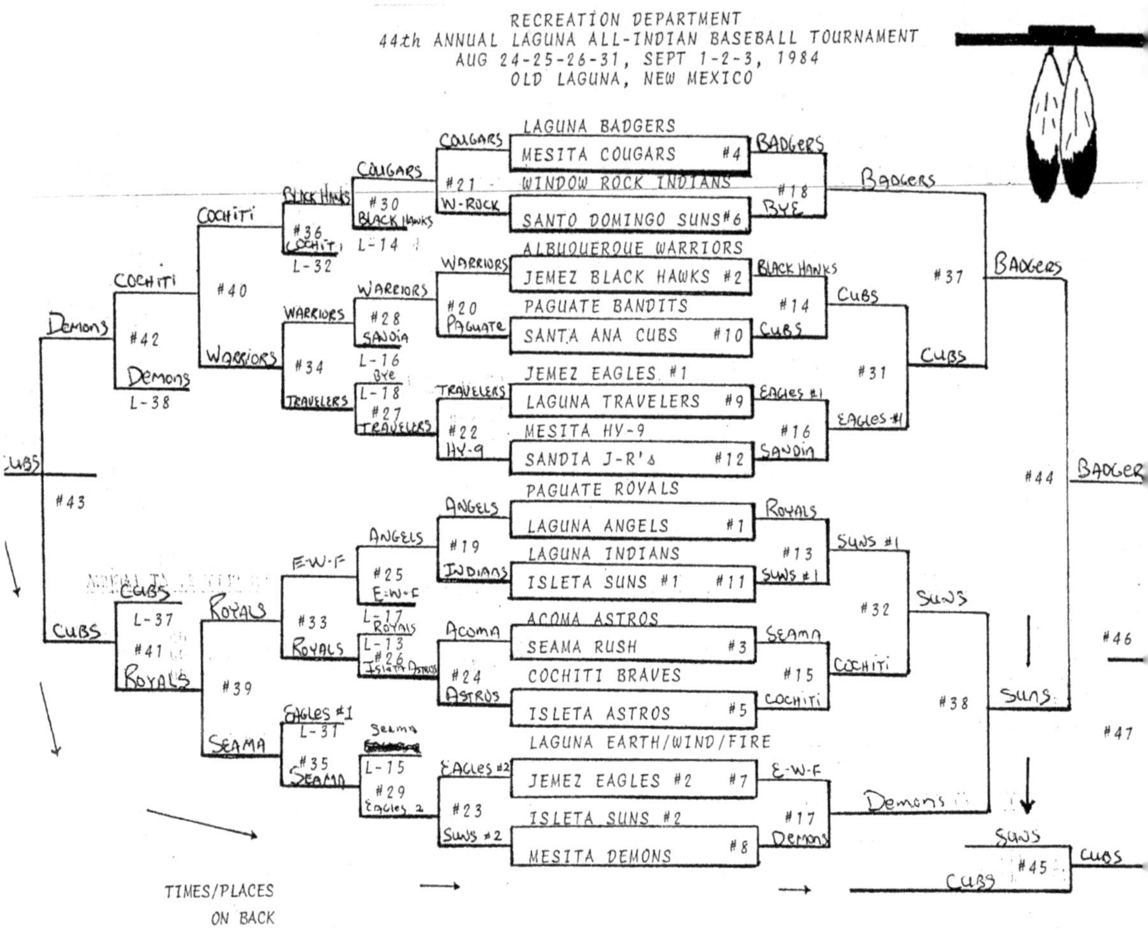

Tournament bracket (handwritten annotations):

LAGUNA BADGERS
MESITA COUGARS #4
WINDOW ROCK INDIANS #21
SANTO DOMINGO SUNS #6
ALBUQUERQUE WARRIORS
JEMEZ BLACK HAWKS #2
PAGUATE BANDITS #20
SANTA ANA CUBS #10
JEMEZ EAGLES #1
LAGUNA TRAVELERS #9
MESITA HV-9 #22
SANDIA J-R's #12
PAGUATE ROYALS
LAGUNA ANGELS #1
LAGUNA INDIANS #19
ISLETA SUNS #1 #11
ACOMA ASTROS
SEAMA RUSH #3
COCHITI BRAVES #24
ISLETA ASTROS #5
LAGUNA EARTH/WIND/FIRE
JEMEZ EAGLES #2 #7
ISLETA SUNS #2 #23
MESITA DEMONS #8

Bracket annotations: COUGARS, BADGERS, BLACK HAWKS, COCHITI, WARRIORS, CUBS, DEMONS, TRAVELERS, ROYALS, ANGELS, INDIANS, SUNS #1, E-W-F, SEAMA, EAGLES #1, EAGLES #2, SUNS #2, ASTROS, ACOMA, W-ROCK, HV-9, SANDIA, BYE

Game numbers: #30, #36, #40, #42, #28, #34, #18, #14, #37, #31, #16, #13, #25, #33, #39, #35, #32, #38, #41, #43, #44, #45, #46, #47, #19, #22, #24, #26, #29, #23, #17, #15

L-32, L-14, L-16, L-18, L-38, L-37, L-17, L-13, L-15, L-3T

TIMES/PLACES
ON BACK

This is the bracket for the 44th annual Laguna All-Indian Baseball Tournament. The tournament, with 24 teams representing Arizona and New Mexico, was held over two weekends at Laguna's various fields in 1984. Many of the listed teams are no longer active or were traveling teams formed specifically for this tournament. This long tradition has sadly disappeared. (Courtesy of Laguna Pueblo.)

This list of teams for the 2014 season includes 24 teams. They played a full season, from early May to early September, including the season-ending tournaments. This season, the South Pueblo League was divided into two divisions: A and B. Most competition takes place within a team's designated division. Two new teams were late additions, the Laguna Heat and the Sandia Hawkeyes. (Courtesy of James Baker.)

| PUEBLO SOUTHERN LEAGUE 2014 SEASON | |
| --- | --- |
| Cochiti Pueblo (2) | Cochiti Braves |
| | Cochiti Dukes |
| Santa Ana Pueblo (3) | Santa Ana Athletics |
| | Santa Ana Cubs |
| | Santa Ana Nakonas |
| Laguna/Acoma/Mesita(5) | Demons |
| | Laguna Monarchs |
| | Horned Frogs |
| | Bombers |
| | Laguna Heat |
| Jemez Pueblo (8) | Pueblo Rays |
| | Jemez Eagles |
| | Hamish Pirates |
| | Jemez Kyotes |
| | Jemez Longhorns |
| | Jemez Sun Devils |
| | Jemez Mets |
| | Jemez Hawks |
| Sandia Pueblo (2) | Sandia Blue Jays |
| | Sandia Hawkeyes |
| Santo Domingo Pueblo | Padres |
| Isleta Pueblo | Toros |

## Northern Pueblo League

### 2014

Tesuque     *Rangers*

Santa Clara     *Braves*

San Ildefonso     *Tewas*

Ohkay Owingeh

- *Angels*

- *Destroyers*

- *Eagles*

- *Dodgers*

The 2014 North Pueblo League had eight teams listed at the beginning of the season. Although numbers have diminished over the years, the level of competition has remained high. Gone are teams like Nambe Falls, the San Juan Yankees, Taos, and the Cochiti Rockies. The North Pueblo League won the 2013 North/South championship and the 2014 North/South All-Star Game. (Courtesy of James Baker.)

Southern Pueblo League 2014 Schedule

**COCHITI**

**Dukes**

A's @ Dukes: May 11, 2014 11am

Longhorns @ Dukes: May 18, 2014 11am

Dukes @ Rays: May 24, 2014 11am

Dukes @ Pirates: June 1, 2014 TBA

Kyotes @ Dukes: June 8, 2014 11am

Dukes @ Giants: June 15, 2014 2pm

Hawkeyes @ Dukes: June 22, 2014 2pm

Blue Jays @ Dukes: June 29, 2014 11am

Dukes @ Eagles: July 6, 2014 2pm

Demons @ Dukes: July 13, 2014 2pm

Isleta @ Dukes: July 20, 2014 11am

TBA: July 27, 2014

**Braves**

Hawks @ Braves: May 11, 2014 2pm

Monarchs @ Braves: May 18, 2014 2pm

Mets @ Braves: May 25, 2014 2pm

Braves @ Padres: June 1, 2014 2pm

Heat@ Braves: June 8, 2014 2pm

Braves @ Bombers: June 15, 2014 2pm

Braves @ HFrogs: June 22, 2014 2pm

Shown here is an example of the master schedule for the 2014 South Pueblo League. Each team has 12 scheduled league games during the four-month season. Under certain circumstances, like the annual feast days, games have to be postponed and made up at a later time. Each team's win/loss record is the primary tool for establishing the seedings for the annual South League Tournament, which takes place in August. The more games a team wins, the better the chances of initial advancement in the brackets. Those initial advantages tend to vanish, however, as emotion and stress during the tournament leads to the possibility of any team beating any other team on a given day. Teams are eliminated after two losses. (Courtesy of Pueblo South League president Dominic Gachupin.)

Fort Marcy Park, formed from an old stone structure, is located just outside of downtown in Santa Fe. A central location for the meeting of the North and South teams, it has hosted numerous North/South All-Star Games and championships over the years. The field is an odd configuration, with a very short fence in right field and a spacious outfield in both left field and center field. The advantage goes to left-handed power hitters. (Photograph by James Baker.)

Pat Kiska is an Albuquerque-based umpire with over 30 years' experience in high school baseball, city adult summer leagues, local Mexican leagues, and championship and all-star Pueblo games. He has also officiated at the annual Pueblo/Navajo games. He has umpired numerous state high school tournaments. Kiska came to Albuquerque from El Paso, Texas. (Photograph by Alice Kiska, courtesy of Herb Howell.)

This Jemez base umpire covers the middle of the field in his role as the visiting-team umpire. He travels with his local Jemez Hawks team. Then, at Hawks home games, he calls the balls and strikes from behind the plate, as tradition has it. (Photograph by James Baker.)

Herb Howell began his umpiring career in San Diego, California, then in Portland, Oregon, before moving to New Mexico and umpiring the South Pueblo League. He has umpired local high school, collegiate, and adult-league baseball and has officiated in Mexico and China. Howell umpired three state high school all-star games in New Mexico. He has served the South All Indian Pueblo League in numerous championship and all-star games since 1993. (Photograph by Alice Kiska, courtesy of Herb Howell.)

Tony Herrera serves as the plate umpire in this Cochiti Braves game. He is also the coach of the Braves, as well as the Cochiti Middle School team. As a former player and now the parent of a player, he represents all aspects of the game of baseball in the South League. (Photograph by James Baker.)

# 5

# THE PUEBLOS

The Pueblo people have been in New Mexico for around 800 years. The layout of New Mexico's pueblos follows the water sources of the Rio Grande and Rio Puerco Rivers in central and northern New Mexico. The land is dry, and rainfall is rare most times of the year. The mountains provide winter snows and wild game for the hunting seasons. Most of the pueblos are in river valleys, which provide the vital water to villages and for the crops of these primarily agrarian communities.

Contact with the outside world was limited to the Navajo Nation to the west and the Apache Nation to the south. From the east came Comanche and Kiowa visitors, who traveled for trade, but also for raiding at harvest times. These small village nations have cultivated the same areas for hundreds of years. The influence of European cultures did not come until the 16th century, with gold-seeking Spanish colonizers.

The influence of the United States was not felt until the area was annexed as a result of the Mexican War in 1848. The US military presence was evident in 1846 with the entrance of Stephan Kearney and his troops. The Santa Fe Trail brought Anglo masses west to seek their fortunes.

It is difficult to generalize about all pueblos based on the knowledge of one pueblo and its daily life. Common themes related to the sense of unity and family, which seeks harmony as a primary value. The village is like a big family, punctuated by clans. The close-knit community shares daily activities broken down by men's and women's roles. The women manage activities related to the home, to children, and to food preparation. The men's roles are mostly outside the home in a wider range of activities, from hunting and gathering to growing of crops and establishing vital irrigation sources. Annual feast day activities of dancing, prayer, and food preparation are divided as well.

Baseball in the pueblos began about 1900, at Isleta, where players completed with local Hispanic village teams and mining company teams along the Rio Grande. Eventually, Pueblo teams played in Albuquerque leagues, as there were no other Pueblo teams playing baseball in the area.

Early development of baseball in the pueblos was gradual and came under outside influences, including Indian schools, the military, the railroads, and mining companies. Pueblo baseball has grown to include as many as 32 teams in the two leagues, and the game still is growing. Of note has been the emergence of Yankee and former Red Sox star Jacoby Ellsbury. He is Native American (Navajo and Yaqui), hailing from New Mexico. His presence in Major League Baseball gives young Pueblo baseball players a role model to watch on television every summer.

Isleta means "little island," but the pueblo is hardly small, as it comprises over 211,000 acres. Isleta has a troubled past, relating to the Pueblo Revolt of 1680. The pueblo was abandoned, with some residents moving west to Hopi lands, while others retreated to El Paso. Today, Isleta is two small communities. This classic Isleta team photograph, dating to 1900, depicts the first known Pueblo village team. Early teams played local non-Indian village teams in regular Sunday games along the Central Rio Grande Valley as far south as Socorro and as far north as Santa Fe. Early Isleta teams were called the Suns, Toros, and Bees. As competition expanded, Isleta teams played in the Albuquerque City Leagues and against mining village teams sponsored by the Northern New Mexico Company. The rich history of Isleta baseball expanded to neighboring Laguna Pueblo and to years of participation in the annual all-Indian tournament there. (Courtesy of Jimmy Abeita.)

THE PUEBLOS

The new green turf stands out against the high-desert surroundings of central New Mexico, where Isleta has thrived for hundreds of years. This showpiece ballpark is an outstanding venue for Isleta Toros' home games and tournament play. This field's condition is in stark contrast with most of the other pueblo baseball fields along the Rio Grande. It is not necessarily better in the view of many players, who claim that on grass infields the bounce of ground balls are more erratic and less predictable than on the soft, dusty dirt fields in most other pueblos. Another drawback of this fine field is the old irrigation ditch behind the spectator seating area. A foul ball hit into the ditch will quickly absorb moisture and become almost unplayable. Sometimes, scrambling kids, in pursuit of the foul ball, tumble into the shallow waters, requiring a quick rescue by an observant adult. (Both photographs by Herb Howell.)

Isleta Pueblo's newly built baseball diamond features a green grass field, with carefully etched base paths and sturdy, modern fencing. When entering the baseball complex from the dusty dirt, one is startled by the contrasts. In addition, the "Watch for snakes" sign is a reminder of the dangers of this desert environment. The sign, not intended as a joke, reflects reality in this otherwise barren landscape. The field is located a few miles east of the main Pueblo village and across the winding Rio Grande River. (Photograph by Herb Howell.)

Jimmy Abeita is one of the knowledgeable elders in Isleta. He provided the 1900 photograph on page 50, identified the shinny photo, and is a general source of information about both baseball and shinny. (Photograph by James Baker.)

THE PUEBLOS

The old Catholic church on the Isleta Pueblo, dating to the 1680s, is evidence of Spanish missionary work in the New Mexico pueblos. The church is centrally located in the Isleta village. It has been maintained and continually restored to the highest standards and its original splendor. (Photograph by James Baker.)

Laguna Pueblo is very large, with around 8,000 members scattered among its six major villages. Residents place a high value on education, having developed their own scholarship program for those seeking a college education and beyond. Ranching has been a traditional occupation, together with mechanical trades and uranium mining. Traditional pottery making has been revitalized. The old Laguna village is seen here from the hill just outside the historic Catholic church. The scenic church is often photographed from I-40 going from Albuquerque to Gallup, New Mexico. (Photograph by Herb Howell.)

The old blue press box and shade shelter sits behind home plate at the renowned ballpark at old Laguna. This field is scenically situated to look directly toward the spiritual Mount Taylor. (Photograph by Herb Howell.)

This backstop is adjacent to the Mesita Village ball field on the Laguna Pueblo. This diamond is but one of many local village fields. At one time, each of the six Laguna villages had its own team and dirt ball field. (Photograph by Herb Howell.)

This is the view, from home plate, of the Mesita Village baseball field. The north-facing photograph shows the scenic red mesa that rises beyond the field. (Photograph by Herb Howell.)

Santa Ana Pueblo is a farming community with an unknown original location. Here, winter is evident only by the barren trees that surround the baseball field. The leaves and tumbleweeds are as much a part of the New Mexico pueblo landscape as the rich blue sky. This area generally gets less than eight inches of rain per year and is often beset with strong winds, usually from the west in the late afternoon. Dust storms do not stop the baseball games; the players forge ahead. The nearby crops are not generally dependent on rain, but rather on the irrigation ditches called *acaquias*. These intricate systems of ditches and small dams are hundreds of years old. The word "acaquia" derives from the similar irrigation systems of old Spain. (Photograph by Herb Howell.)

THE PUEBLOS

The villages are spread throughout Santa Ana Pueblo, just east of the Rio Grande River. People have occupied this area since 1700. The farming equipment and work vehicles are kept at the homes of local farmers and shared among the various families and neighbors. The fields and irrigation ditches are but a few yards away from each other. Lawns are not grown, as it is seen as a waste of precious water that can be put to better use for crops. Native vegetation is the normal ground cover, requiring no maintenance. The tumbleweeds arrive and depart with the wind. (Both photographs by Herb Howell.)

San Felipe Giants players sit during a game at Santa Ana, along with one of the player's younger brother. This photograph displays the close-knit family nature of baseball in the New Mexico pueblos. The young boy watches, learns, and awaits his opportunity to play Pueblo baseball with his cousins and older brothers. (Photograph by Herb Howell.)

Sandia Bluejays players discuss strategy in the late afternoon at the Santa Ana field. Here, the team is competing against the old Cochiti Brewers. The Brewers were leading 5-4, with one out in the bottom of the ninth. The base runner, Sandia catcher Lance Bernal, executed a perfect squeeze bunt to drive in the tying run. The next batter bunted Bernal to second base on a sacrifice, making the second out. A wild pitch followed, moving Bernal to third. This photograph captures that crucial point of the game. Would Sandia bunt again? The position of the Cochiti third baseman indicates just that. Sure enough, the Bluejays bunted for a third time. Bernal scored the winning run for a thrilling 6-5 victory! (Photograph by Herb Howell.)

The Rio Grande River is central to ancient Tamaya/Santa Ana and its land holdings, both east and west of the river. This long river begins in the Colorado Mountains and winds down the middle of New Mexico, cutting valleys and gorges as it flows. The river is the feeder of life, giving water to the acaquia system of irrigation canals that feed the agricultural areas for most of the pueblos along its 1,500-mile descent. (Photograph by Herb Howell.)

JEMEZ EAGLES
ALL INDIAN
MEN'S BASEBALL TOURNAMENT
50TH ANNIVERSARY
1957-2007

Sept. 22, 23 & 29, 30 2007

4 Day Event

Pre-register by: ASAP

ENTRY FEE:
• $ 200.00 ($ 100
DEPOSIT TO RESERVE
SPOT) 12 TEAM
DOUBLE-ELIMINATION
20 PLAYER PER ROSTER

Deadline Sept. 21, 2007

The games will be held @ Middle
field
And Lower Field

Dedicated to all former players and
deceased

For more information or to register call:

Contact person: Verman (505)
834-0657
(505) 948-0266

**Awards**

Championship
Team
2nd place Team
3rd place Team
4th place Team
MVP Awards
All Tourney Team
Sportsmanship
Award

**Planning
Committee**

Jemez Eagles
Family

Verman
Romero Family

Robert Shendo
Family

Lionel Romero
Family

Bill Fragua
Family

Jemez Pueblo is a closed village and only allows visitors on feast days. This condition exists out of respect for the privacy of those who live there. The feast days are not publicized due to capacity issues. The poster shown at left advertises the 2007 Jemez Eagles All Indian Men's Baseball Tournament, which commemorated 50 years of the Jemez baseball team. This special tournament was played after the regular season and the annual north/south playoffs. The Eagles were the prominent team, with competition from other pueblo teams. The Jemez Pueblo has the largest number of teams in the South Pueblo League, with eight. The T-shirt shown below lists the names of Eagle players who have passed away over the years. (Both photographs by Herb Howell.)

IN MEMORY OF:
FORMER PLAYERS

ALFRED CASIQUITO SR.
EDWARD "22" CASIQUITO
BENJI ZUNI
EMO JR. YEPA
JOSEPH DANIEL CASIQUITO
DANIEL C. ROMERO SR.
DANIEL CURTIS ROMERO JR.
JULIAN TAFOYA
NOAL COLAQUE
TIMOTHY TAFOYA
IVAN "SPOOK" FRAGUA
IVAN ARMIJO
DAVID MAGDALENA
FRANK C. WAQUIE

ERNIE TOSA
ANDY LORRETTO
PATRICK WAQUIE
PABLO CHINANA
TELASFOR LORRETTO
WILBURT BACA
JOSE WAQUIE
HENRY MORA
MANUEL "BUCK" WAQUIE
RANDOLF PADILLA
JOSEPH SABUQUIE
ROY GACHUPIN
ROBERT FRAGUA

1957 - 2007

At right, a deer and a man are linked symbolically by Jemez artist and baseball leader Bob Shendo. He played baseball at his native home of Taos Pueblo before moving to Jemez Pueblo after his marriage to a Jemez woman. He helped form the Jemez Eagles baseball team and has remained with the club for well over 50 years as a player (first base), coach, and supporter. In the photograph above, Shendo (left), poses with Jemez teammates Al Summer (center) and Tom Summer after a game in 1984 at Jemez Pueblo. (Above, courtesy of Herb Howell; at right, James Baker.)

The local Hamish Pirates and the visiting Cochiti Dukes play the second game of a Sunday doubleheader. Families and players alike seek cover from the midday heat. Children, mothers, grandmothers, and girlfriends sit around and behind their local team. Sometimes, families set up a small concession stand on the back of a pickup truck or under the tarp next to the backstop fence. Snow cones are favorites with the kids, and soft drinks and water are shared with the players a few feet away. After each game, spectators fold up their chairs and tents to make room for the next family of supporters. Traditional local foods are shared with the players. These food items, always home-cooked Jemez fare, feature lots of local red chili. (Photograph by Herb Howell.)

Umpire T.J. Loretto poses at Isotopes Park in Albuquerque prior to the 2007 Pueblos/Navajos All-Star Game. Loretto developed his umpiring skills in Albuquerque as an arbiter of high school baseball games while still a player with the Hamish Pirates of Jemez Pueblo. He has since been chosen to umpire many playoff, championship, and all-star games. Loretto represents a long line of "Jemez umps." Umpires at Jemez often work both men's baseball and women's softball games. Local umpire training is scarce; instead, umpiring mechanics are passed on from one umpire to another. The skills are taught by doing. Most Pueblo Indian umpires are developed in this way after their playing days are over. Very often, they become the coach of their old team and then end up being the home team home-plate umpire for the team they coach. (Photograph by Alex Kiska.)

THE PUEBLOS

Ohkay Owingeh Pueblo, formerly San Juan Pueblo, has a two-part social system comprising the Winter People and the Summer People. Each has its own ceremonies and dances. An important value is that of teaching responsibility. The pueblo is a well-known center for arts and crafts, such as jewelry, pottery, and a variety of other art forms. Shown here is an Ohkay Owingeh championship team from the late 1950s. (Courtesy of Larry Phillips.)

Among the players in this 1960s photograph is Larry Phillips (standing third from left, in background). Since his baseball days, he has become an artist, has taught at the Institute for American Indian Arts for 30 years, and now serves in pueblo management as first lieutenant governor. (Courtesy of Larry Phillips.)

The teams shown here played in the 1970s. Note the small child, front and center, in the photograph below. (Both courtesy of Larry Phillips.)

THE PUEBLOS

Marcelino Aquina is the current governor of the pueblo. In the championship photograph the image below on page 63, he is second from the left in the bottom row. (Photograph by James Baker.)

The baseball field at Ohkay Owingeh is seen here from behind the backstop. The structures shown here are, from left to right, the stands, the backstop, and the visitors' dugout. (Photograph by James Baker.)

The baseball diamond is seen here from right field. (Photograph by James Baker.)

This distance marker is attached to the right-field fence. The field's dimensions are comparable to those of a major-league park. (Photograph by James Baker.)

THE PUEBLOS

Santa Clara Pueblo's diverse attractions include the prehistoric Puye cliff dwellings. Among the outdoor activities available in the pueblo are camping and fishing in the canyons. Santa Clara's scenic land is but one of its benefits, along with a strong tribal government and economy. Residents maintain their tribal heritage and place a high value on educating the youth. Some of their dances and festivals are open to the public each year. This photograph of the playing field for league games was taken from a nearby hilltop. The geologic formation "Black Mesa" can be seen in the distance at right. (Photograph by James Baker.)

The photograph above of the playing field was taken from behind first base. It shows the backstop, team dugouts, and what is probably a concession stand. Below, Charles Suzao stands near the home dugout. At almost all pueblos, a tribal person showed the photographer to the field. (Both photographs by James Baker.)

This softball field stands adjacent to the baseball diamond. Another field in the area (not shown) is used for Little League and youth games. (Photograph by James Baker.)

This baseball was found in the parking lot of the baseball field. Written on it is the inscription "Indians." (Photograph by James Baker.)

Tesuque Pueblo, north of Santa Fe, is one of the most traditional of the pueblos and one of the smallest. This pueblo has existed since before 1200. Residents maintained their traditional rituals and ceremonies despite the invasion of the Spanish and other cultures. Farming and pottery remain primary economic activities. Most Tesuque dances and ceremonies are open to the public. The pueblo's members are noted for the outstanding costumes at their rituals and dances. The pueblo name "Tesuque" is written in white stone just above right field. It can be seen from nearby US 84. (Photograph by James Baker.)

THE PUEBLOS

This photograph of the baseball field was taken from a point near the "Tesuque" marker. It provides a comprehensive view of the facility. (Photograph by James Baker.)

Pictured is the backstop and beyond it, from left to right, the visitors' dugout, a green building, and the stands. (Photograph by James Baker.)

THE PUEBLOS

San Ildefonso is most famous for it black-on-black pottery, which is highly regarded by art collectors. The Pueblo people of San Ildefonso have resided at their location since before the 1200s. They are noted for retaining their ancient traditions, dances, and ceremonies. Education is a high priority, with many of the young people going on to college or another form of advanced education. Shown here is the main playing field. (Photograph by James Baker.)

Shown here is an adjacent, lighted field. It is not currently used for league games. (Photograph by James Baker.)

A large picnic area is provided for spectators to watch the games. The area has six shelters, including the two shown here. (Photograph by James Baker.)

A group of children play baseball in the front yard of a nearby home. (Photograph by James Baker.)

THE PUEBLOS

This little girl, Donicia Lovato, plays near her home. Just before these photographs were taken, she stuck her head through the wire fence and gave the photographer a huge grin! (Both photographs by James Baker.)

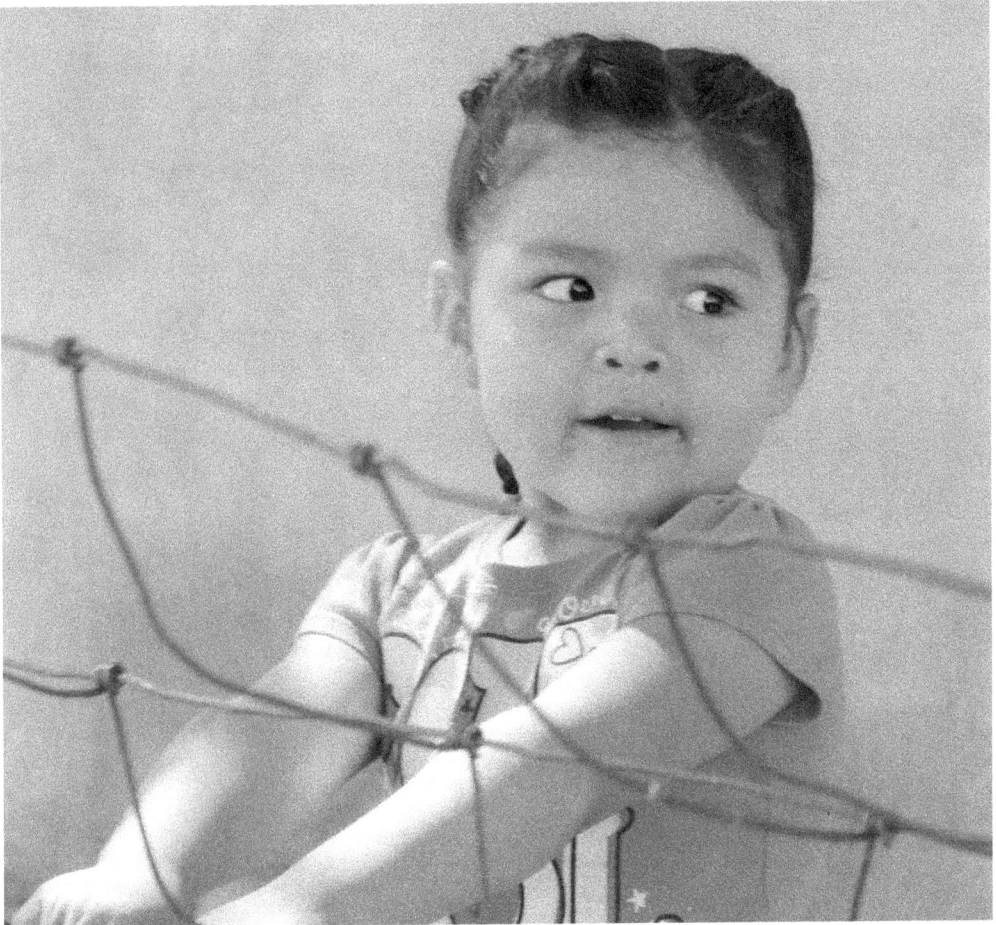

This beautiful San Ildefonso church is located off the plaza area. It was constructed around 1905 on the ruins of a 17th-century mission church. (Photograph by James Baker.)

This is another view of Black Mesa. The photograph was taken just outside the pueblo. (Photograph by James Baker.)

THE PUEBLOS

Sandia Pueblo became a settlement for the Spanish in 1617. It is the least known and least understood of the pueblos. It is small, but it is diverse economically with activity in farming and agriculture. It is the closest pueblo to city life. After a history of early conflict with invaders and resulting abandonment, residents prize their land, which goes from the Rio Grande River to the Sandia Mountains. Sandia Pueblo developed the baseball complex shown here, which has lights, modern chain-link fences, and a grass outfield. This is the first such complex in the South Pueblo League. The photograph shows the modern seating area with a roof to protect spectators from the intense New Mexico summer sun. Such a covering is rare for pueblo ball fields. (Photograph by Herb Howell.)

This photograph, taken from behind the bleachers, offers the spectators' view of the large playing area. Visible beyond the outfield fence are newly developed housing units. (Photograph by Herb Howell.)

This modern dugout's safety features include a high chain-link fence. The dugout has direct access to the parking lot and spectator areas. (Photograph by Herb Howell.)

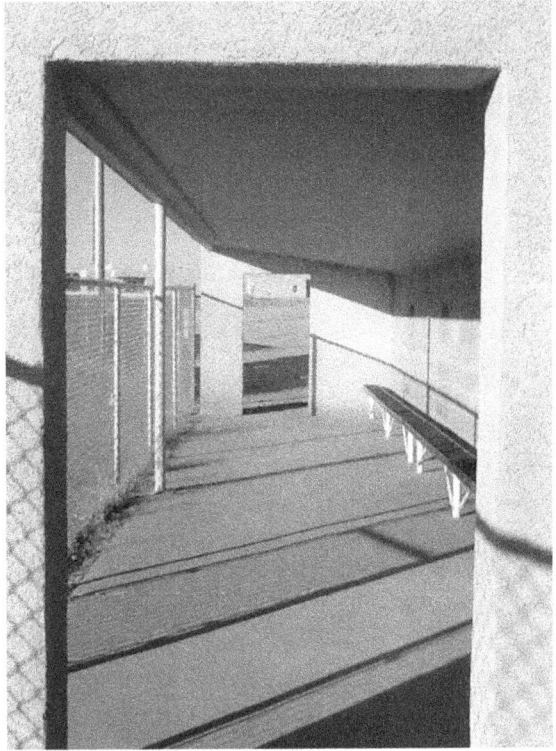

An old building is clearly dated to 1930. It remains an administrative building on the Sandia Pueblo today. Traditional architecture and the tan adobe mud surface endure the hot sun and survive with periodic plastering, thus its original splendor is preserved. To the front of the building (beyond the frame of this photograph) is a classic bread oven, called an *arno*. It is still in use today, near the center of the newly developed sport and recreation complex at Sandia. (Photograph by Herb Howell.)

Santo Domingo, one of the largest pueblos, is also considered the most conservative in its use of culture and maintenance of its customs. Religious structures and customs are at the core of the very closed social structure. Today's crafts are sold successfully with traditional pottery and jewelry making. The photographs on this page depict the Santo Domingo field. There are only small spectator stands, and only one tree protects fans from the sun. (Both photographs by James Baker.)

THE PUEBLOS

The photograph above shows the area of an early playing field. Below is the property after having been cleared for a new baseball field. (Both photographs by James Baker.)

Irvin Coriz is the head of health services, which includes the gym as well as the baseball fields. He notes that the pueblo is now teaching youths to play shinny as a historical game. Students are taught to find and carve their own sticks. He says the game becomes quite rough and that sometimes the players are so involved mixing it up that they do not know where the ball is. (Photograph by James Baker.)

# 6

# PUEBLO/NAVAJO
# ALL-STAR GAME

The Pueblo Leagues feature two all-star games to showcase the top players and their talents. The two leagues, the North and the South, are generally divided geographically by Santa Fe.

The host of the North/South All-Star Game alternates between the northern and southern pueblos. It is held annually on July 4. Managers of the two first-place teams are chosen to lead their respective squads. The various coaches select which players will compete. Since there is no age stipulation, it is often the case that teenagers and men in their 50s play with and against each other, just as they do every weekend. The excitement grows as the players' families and fellow pueblo members come to cheer their local heroes. There is no lack of intensity on the part of the players and the fans alike.

There is a curtain-raiser game, in which the old-timers take the field for a fun competition. The pace is a bit slower, but a good time is had by all. This contest often includes men who played in the feature game years ago.

The second all-star game, also in July, is between the best of the Pueblos and the best of the Navajos. This game is interesting, because the Pueblos and Navajos were historical enemies. The venue is Isotopes Park, the home of the Albuquerque Isotopes, the Triple-A farm club of the Los Angeles Dodgers. The series was started in 2002 by John Koldyke, owner of the Isotopes, and Dominic Gachupin, the president of the South Pueblo League. Their goal was to develop an event that could be a fundraiser for the creation of baseball scholarships for Pueblo players at New Mexico Highland University. The game has been a rousing success, with crowds of noisy spectators celebrating the pride of both the culture and their athletes.

For many players, Isotopes Park is the best facility they will ever use. It is in stark contrast to the dusty fields that exist in the pueblos. At this time, only two pueblos have grass fields.

The photographs in this chapter are from the 2007 all-star game. It was well attended, with over 5,000 spectators enjoying a highly competitive game. The Pueblo all-stars scored the winning run at the very end.

Isotopes Park is a modern and spectacular 15,000-seat ballpark that opened in 2003. This stadium replaced the old Albuquerque Dukes Stadium but retained the original lower bowl. Ground was broken in October 2001 for the facility, which would host the Triple-A, Pacific Coast League franchise that moved from Calgary, Alberta, Canada. The team, originally affiliated with the Florida Marlins, later became a farm team of the Los Angeles Dodgers, as is so today. (Photograph by James Baker.)

This view from the upper deck of Isotopes Park reveals the lower seating area, featuring a large crowd of Native American baseball supporters. These games were the result of collaboration between the Isotopes owner, Mike Koldyke, and Pueblo leadership. Koldyke, who owns a ranch near Las Vegas, New Mexico, wanted to support the Highlands University baseball program. Proceeds from these Native American all-star games have been providing scholarship money for promising baseball players. (Photograph by Randy Siner.)

The Navajo all-star roster displays the variety of player hometowns represented on this select team. A number of those players have college baseball experience. The roster reveals that the players are versatile and able to support their team by playing a variety of positions. (Photograph by Randy Siner.)

## PUEBLO ALL STARS TEAM ROSTER

| # | Name | Positions | Pueblo |
|---|------|-----------|--------|
| 1 | CORY CARRILLO | 2B/3B | LAGUNA PUEBLO |
| 2 | JONATHAN CATA | OF/1B | OHKAY OWINGEH |
| 3 | BEN CHAVEZ | P/1B/OF | LAGUNA PUEBLO |
| 4 | BRYCE GABALDON | 1B/P | OHKAY OWINGEH |
| 5 | WIL FRESQUEZ | 1B/3B/OF | NAMBE PUEBLO |
| 6 | JEREMY "WORM" LEON-SANDERS | SS/3B/2B/OF (Team Co-Captain) | SANTA ANA PUEBLO |
| 7 | JEREMY LITTLEHOOP | P/SS/3B/1B | SAN FELIPE PUEBLO |
| 8 | JONAH LITTLEHOOP | P/SS/3B/1B | SAN FELIPE PUEBLO |
| 9 | LEANDER LORETTO | 3B/OF | JEMEZ PUEBLO |
| 10 | JUAN LUJAN | P/OF/3B | ISLETA PUEBLO |
| 11 | GORMAN ROMERO | P/SS/OF (Team Co-Captain) | JEMEZ PUEBLO |
| 12 | JEREMY OYENQUE | 3B/1B | SANTA CLARA/OHKAY OWINGEH |
| 13 | JUSTIN SANCHEZ | OF/1B | SAN FELIPE PUEBLO |
| 14 | LOUIS SANDOVAL | C/1B | SAN FELIPE PUEBLO |
| 15 | JUSTIN SUINA | C/3B/2B | COCHITI PUEBLO |
| 16 | SEAN TRANCOSA | P/OF/3B | SAN FELIPE PUEBLO |
| 17 | ORLANDO ROMERO | OF/2B | JEMEZ PUEBLO |
| 18 | THUNDER BEAR YATES | OF/2B | TESUQUE PUEBLO/NAMBE |
| 19 | IRWIN PECOS | MANAGER - HEAD COACH | JEMEZ PUEBLO |
| 20 | ALBERT TENORIO | ASSISTANT COACH | SAN FELIPE PUEBLO |
| 21 | TONY HERRERA | ASSISTANT COACH | COCHITI PUEBLO |
| 22 | RANDY RILEY | ASSISTANT COACH | LAGUNA PUEBLO |
| 23 | DOMINIC GACHUPIN | ASSISTANT COACH | JEMEZ PUEBLO |
| 24 | JAMES TENORIO | SCORE KEEPER | SAN FELIPE PUEBLO |

The Pueblo all-star roster shows a great representation from throughout the northern and southern pueblos. As with the Navajo team, these players can perform at multiple positions. Cocaptains for the team were Jemez pitcher Gorman Romero and Santa Ana infielder Jeremy Leon-Sanders. These two players were the first recipients of the Highlands University baseball scholarships. (Photograph by Randy Siner.)

Santa Ana Pueblo player Jeremy Leon-Sanders, also a Pueblo all-star second baseman, shows respect and friendship as he shakes hands with an unidentified Navajo first baseman. Pueblo all-star assistant coach Tony Herrera, of Cochiti Pueblo, is on the far right. (Photograph by Randy Siner.)

Jemez Pueblo's Gorman Romero prepares to fire another of his renowned 90-mile-per-hour fastballs. His talents were later displayed at New Mexico Highlands University. (Photograph by Randy Siner.)

Pueblo supporters display feathers and war clubs to add to the festive atmosphere. This was a particularly noisy crowd. A traditional drum group also in attendance had sung prior to the start of the game. (Both photographs by Randy Siner.)

On this day, rain fell during the contest. In the photograph above, umbrellas are being held by those who chose to brave the elements and stay in their seats. The majority of the crowd moved under the shelter of the upper decks. Below, spectators can be seen sitting under plastic tarps. Even in inclement weather, the game continued. (Both photographs by Randy Siner.)

After scoring the game-winning run in the bottom of the 10th inning, Jeremy Leon-Sanders joins family and Santa Ana spectators (below) to celebrate the victory over the Navajo All-Stars. Prior to scoring the winning run, Leon-Sanders (above) was on second base with two outs. When a grounder was hit to the infield, he sprinted to third base and then toward home plate, although an out seemed certain. But, the throw to first base was low, and the ball was not fielded cleanly. The batter was safe at first, and Leon-Sanders raced toward home plate, sliding dramatically. He was ruled safe after a late tag by the catcher. Game over! Pueblos win! (Both photographs by Randy Siner.)

The winning Pueblo all-stars proudly pose with their winning trophy. This traveling trophy goes home with the winning team each year and then is brought back to be defended the next year. These tired players have already changed into their street shoes for the trip home. In most cases, the same players will be competing for their respective pueblo teams the next afternoon. These proud moments will never be forgotten. (Photograph by Randy Siner.)

# THE COCHITI BRAVES

The Cochiti Pueblo is unique in that there is enough information available to gain a detailed history of over 80 years.

Cochiti does not have the oldest team; that honor belongs to Isleta. The earliest Cochiti baseball photographs are from 1933. The first competitive team is believed to have been the Redskins. A 1948 team photograph is included in this chapter. The second team was the Braves, which became the mainstay of the pueblo. Other teams would come and go, such as the Brewers and the Dukes. Today, the Dukes are the current second team.

Historically, the Braves have been a remarkably successful team. Many at Cochiti believe the Braves' record for wins and championships will never be surpassed. This high level of achievement seems to come from the vision and effort of Sam Arquero. His focus was on the youth, many of whom were not allowed to play for the Redskins because the team roster was full. Thus, the Braves were formed and quickly became a championship team under the direction of Arquero. He then became the baseball coach at Santa Fe Indian School. During his tenure, the teams won the New Mexico state championship once and came in second place twice. Since most of the players at that time were from Cochiti, this meant a steady stream of talented players returning to Cochiti to play for the Braves.

This is the earliest known photograph, in 1933, of a Cochiti team. The third man from the right is Marcello Quintana, who was an exceptional player and leader of baseball in the pueblo. (Courtesy of Marie Cordero.)

This is a restored version of the 1933 photograph above. (Restoration by James Baker.)

THE COCHITI BRAVES

This 1948 team is the Redskins, thought to be the first Cochiti team to play in the Pueblo Leagues. (Courtesy of Patricia Lange.)

The early field used by the Redskins was located by the windmill. This is currently how the area looks. (Photograph by James Baker.)

Sam Arquero has been a fundamental force in Cochiti baseball for nearly 70 years. It was his vision and implementation, with the help of others, that led the early Braves to be an elite team, and they sustained this level for several decades. He coached Santa Fe Indian School to the state high school finals three times, coming away a winner once. His coaching provided a steady flow of well-educated baseball talent back to the Pueblo Leagues and to Cochiti Pueblo. His sons picked up a deep knowledge of the game, having been raised by this great man. (Photograph by James Baker.)

A legendary figure in Pueblo baseball is Joseph "Shramee" Quintana, pictured here with his son Jeremy. Joseph tells many stories of baseball's history in the area. One is about the catcher who made his own mask out of wire. Another tale concerns an altercation during one of the championship tournament games, which led to a shooting. And, finally, Shramee tells of a crucial game in which he, at more than 60 years of age, was asked to play because there were not enough Braves players. Shramee played first base because he could not throw or run well. During the game, he got three hits off of the opposing pitcher, a player for Arizona State University. Shramee played and coached baseball his entire life. As seen in this photograph, he lives for the game. His father, Cochiti baseball pioneer Marcello Quintana, taught the game's traditions well. Shramee is doing the same for the current generation of Braves players. Cochiti baseball is his family. (Photograph by Marie Cordero.)

The senior Pueblo members are especially important because they had early experiences and heard stories from relatives of even earlier days. Elder Joseph Benado (pictured) was helpful in establishing the Braves. He speaks of a Cochiti team called the Silversmiths. Little information has been found about this group. (Photograph by James Baker.)

Posing here are Gerald Chavez and his wife, Opal. Gerald played during the early 1950s. He and Joseph Benado have memories of the great championship game in which the Braves played an outstanding (maybe undefeated) Tesuque team and won 19-0. They also particularly enjoyed playing inmates in the New Mexico State Penitentiary in Santa Fe. Chavez likes to recall the game in which he struck out 19 batters (or maybe 17 . . . or 18). (Photograph by James Baker.)

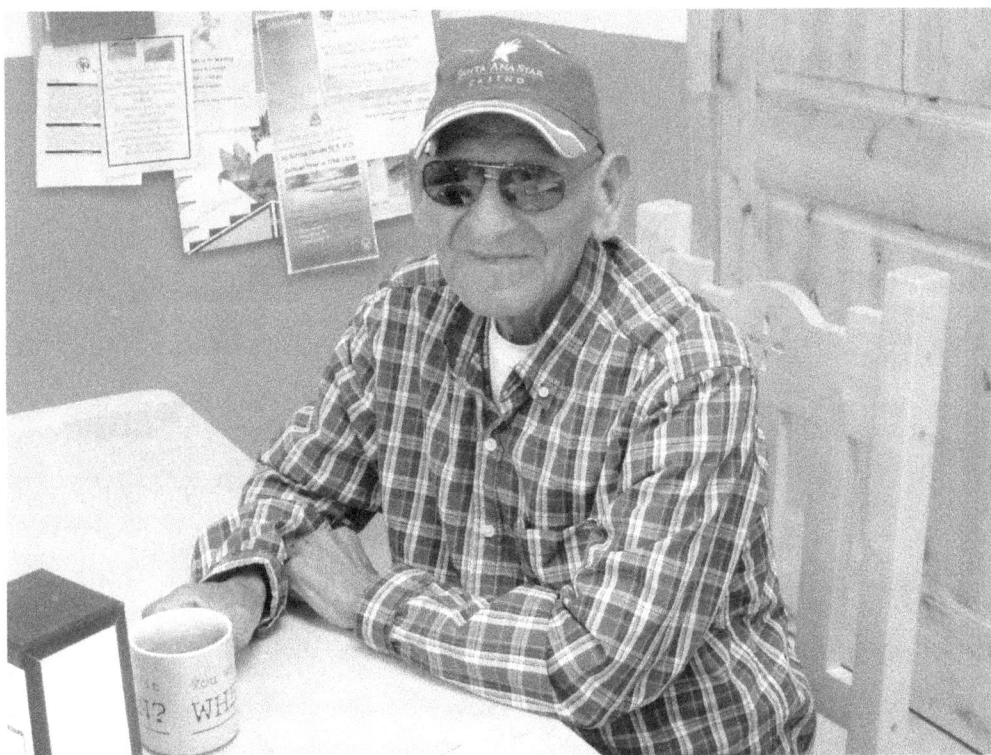

Shown above is elder John Quintana. He recalled the years the Braves won three championships in a row (1954–1956) that allowed the Braves to keep the traveling trophy. The Braves are the only team that has ever accomplished this feat. Pictured below is Ulee Quintana. These men are among several who remarked how great it was to play the New Mexico State Penitentiary prisoners, and that when they did, the inmates who were spectators cheered for the Braves. (Both photographs by James Baker.)

These are two Braves championship teams from the 1950s. This is the period of the big championship game against Tesuque, which the Braves won 19-0. It was also the time when teams traveled to play the inmates at the New Mexico State Penitentiary. (Both courtesy of Marie Cordero.)

This is another Braves championship team of the late 1950s or early 1960s. (Courtesy of Marie Cordero.)

Photographs of daily life inside the New Mexico prisons are quite rare. There is a bleacher area on the left of the photograph above. Below is a zoomed-in version of the far right of the photograph above, created by Hanna Abelbeck. It clearly shows the activity to be a baseball game. The image dates to the 1950s. (Both courtesy of Palace of Governors Photo Archives, 073471.)

THE COCHITI BRAVES

Here is an old Cochiti baseball field in the mid-1970s. Both images are taken from the backstop, which was made of chicken wire. The cooler seen below was for spectators to store beverages for consumption during the game. (Both courtesy of Marie Cordero.)

The bench for the home team is pictured above, and the visitors bench is below. In these and in the photographs on the previous page, there is no evidence of an outfield fence. (Both courtesy of Marie Cordero.)

The construction of an outfield fence is shown here. The photograph dates to the 1970s. (Courtesy of Marie Cordero.)

These are championship teams of the 1970s (above) and the 1990s (below). (Both courtesy of Marie Cordero.)

THE COCHITI BRAVES

From 1970 to 1990, the Braves maintained a level of excellence. This was due in part to exceptional players and managers. Gilbert Herrera (at right) played for the Braves for many years. He is shown here playing for the US Navy at Treasure Island. Silviano Quintana (below) managed for several years. (Both courtesy of Marie Cordero.)

Here is Cochiti Pueblo from the air. The two adjacent baseball fields are visible at the upper center of the image. (Photograph by James Baker.)

This is Cochiti Pueblo shown from Highway 22. The mountains beyond the pueblo offer an attractive setting. (Photograph by James Baker.)

The sign above designates the entrance to the Cochiti Reservation. Below, the governor's office and administration building is a modern Pueblo structure. (Both photographs by James Baker.)

THE COCHITI BRAVES

These photographs show Braves Field in 2013 and 2014. Above, the infield is seen from left field. The image below was taken from outside the playing field, near first base. Structures seen here are, from left to right, the visitors' bench, the backstop, the concession area, some bleachers, and the home dugout. (Both photographs by James Baker.)

The field area is seen in the photograph above, taken at the edge of the bleachers and looking toward left field. Below is the field from behind the Braves' dugout. (Both photographs by James Baker.)

THE COCHITI BRAVES

Shown on this page are the dugouts at Braves Field. The home team (Braves) uses the dugout seen above; the visitors' dugout is below. Joseph Quintana relates that, in the beginning, the dugouts were both of concrete construction. But, over time, tree roots caused the concrete of the visitors' dugout to break and crumble. It was replaced with a wood structure. (Both photographs by James Baker.)

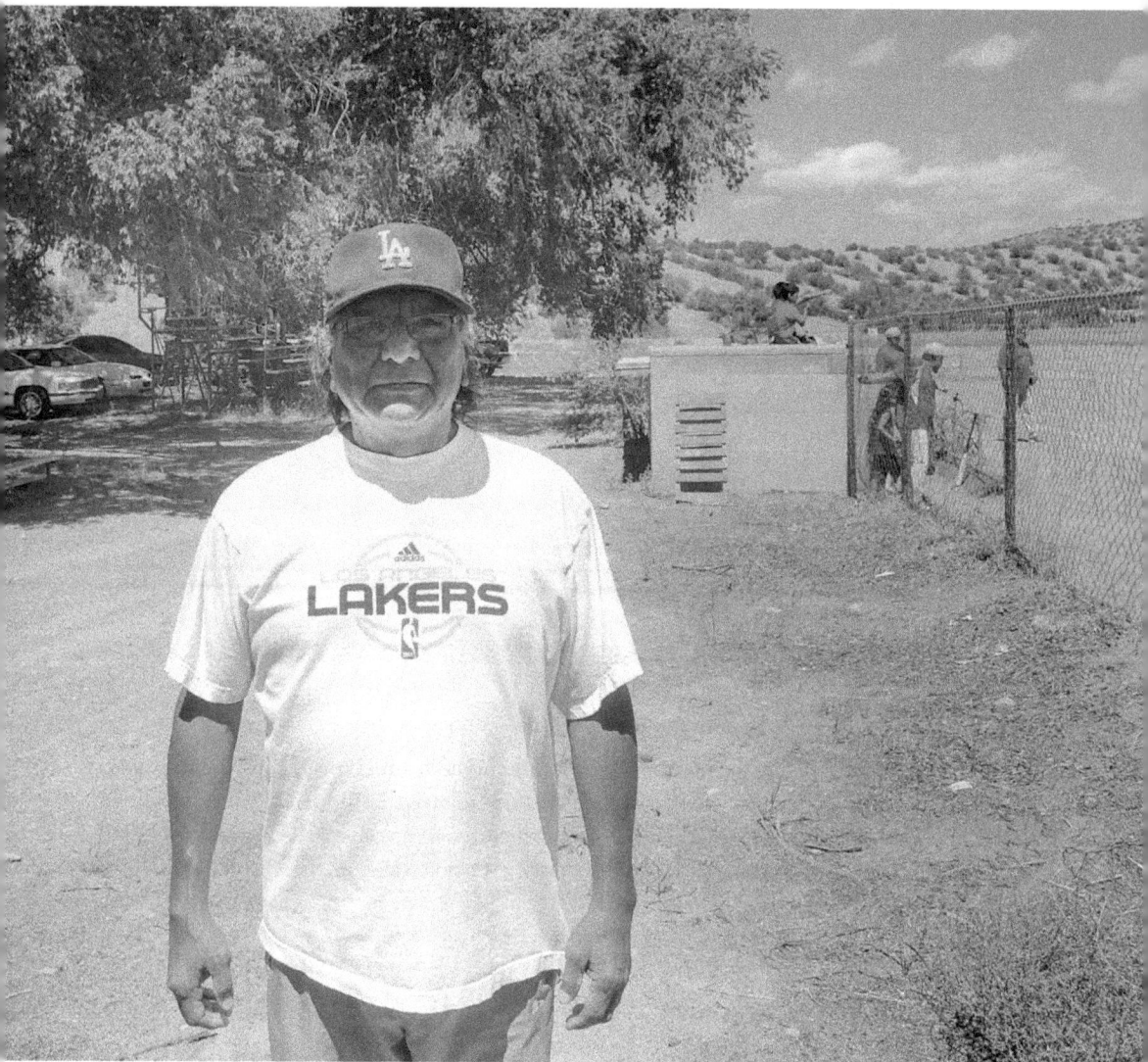

After watching both the Cochiti Dukes and the Cochiti Braves play on June 8, 2014, Herb Howell wrote this about Tony Herrera (pictured): "Here is the man who showed up early to provide field-lining equipment for the other Cochiti team [Dukes], raked the field, then did it all again for his team (Braves) three hours later, prepared his team to play, then umpired the nine-inning game. First to arrive and last to leave; every Sunday for years." (Photograph by James Baker.)

These photographs were taken at a 2012 game between the Cochiti Braves and the Jemez Hawks. Above, Braves players take a short break. Below, Hawks players wait to bat. (Both photographs by James Baker.)

These photographs were during the same game as seen on the previous page. Above, a Braves pitcher throws to a Hawks batter. Shown at left is a Braves player taking a "mighty swing." The batter swung and missed. (Both photographs by James Baker.)

Everyone contributes to baseball games in the pueblos. In this case, Marie Cordero serves as the official scorer at a Braves game in 2012. (Photograph by James Baker.)

Children are an integral part of the game environment. They learn by practicing and watching. Here, a small boy plays catch near home plate. (Photograph by James Baker.)

There is no fee for admission to the games. The Braves use bingo parties (at left) as a source of revenue to provide the team with uniforms and equipment. Another method for raising money is food sales (below) at various homes. (At left, photograph by Marie Cordero; below, photograph by James Baker.)

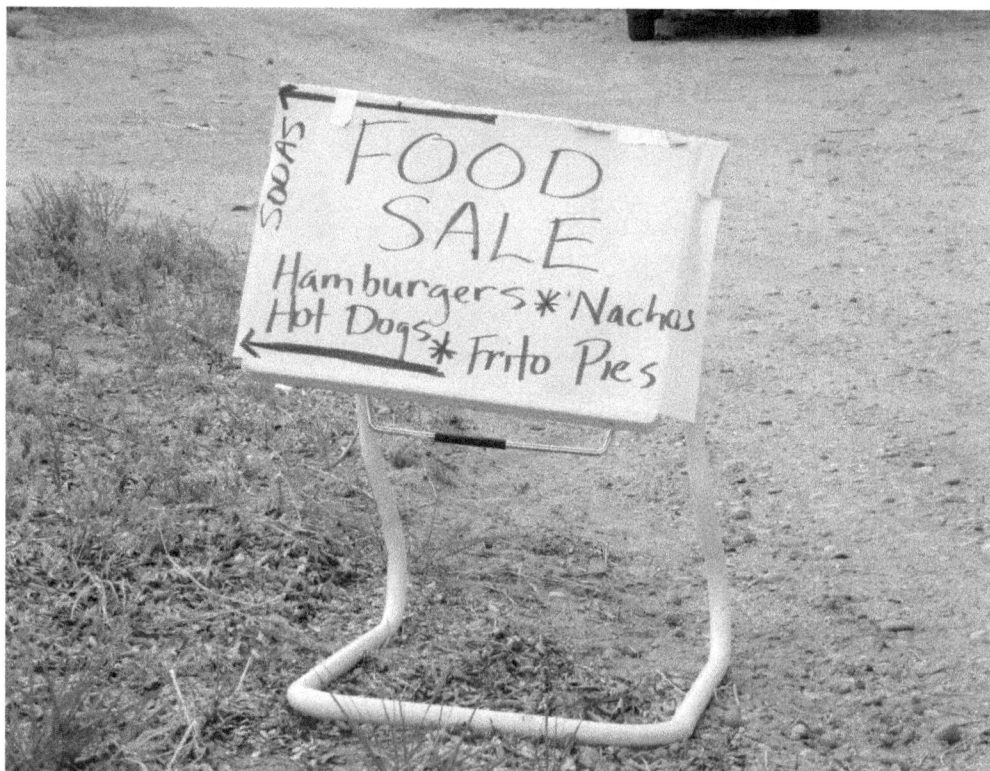

SODAS

FOOD SALE
Hamburgers * Nachos
Hot Dogs * Frito Pies

# Baseball Family
## (Marie Cordero)

| Grandfather | Father | Uncle | Brother | Nephew |
|---|---|---|---|---|
| *Marcello Quintana* | *Gilbert Herrera* | *Joseph Quintana* | *Tony Herrera* | *Jared Quintana* |
| Played baseball on first Cochiti teams | Played for Braves | Played for Braves | Played for Braves | Plays for Braves |
| Exceptional player | Played for US Navy (Treasure Island) | Played well past 55 years of age | Coaches Braves | Pitched Opening Game 2014 |
| Coached original Braves | | Considered baseball guru | Umpires League Games | |
| | | | Coached Pueblo All-Stars | |

**Grandsons**

All four play baseball
Gene was 2014 North/ South All-Star

Family is the historical foundation of pueblo teams—it has been that way for decades. A portion of the baseball family of Marie Cordero is shown here. The family baseball tree now extends to five generations. (Courtesy of James Baker.)

Continuing their remarkable tradition, the Braves are shown here after winning the 2013 South Division championship. The Braves lost to the Ohkay Owingeh team in the North/South championship game. (Photograph by Marie Cordero.)

While the Braves have been the main Cochiti team, there often is a second team. It is currently the Cochiti Dukes. There is a second field, sometimes used by the Dukes, located adjacent to Braves Field. Shown here is the inside of the home dugout. Currently, both teams use Braves Field. (Photograph by James Baker.)

Shown here is the second field formerly used by the Dukes. The view is from outside the field, looking in. Both dugouts and the backstop are visible. (Photograph by James Baker.)

Here, two players from the Cochiti Dukes warm up for a game with the Jemez Kyotes during the 2014 season. (Photograph by James Baker.)

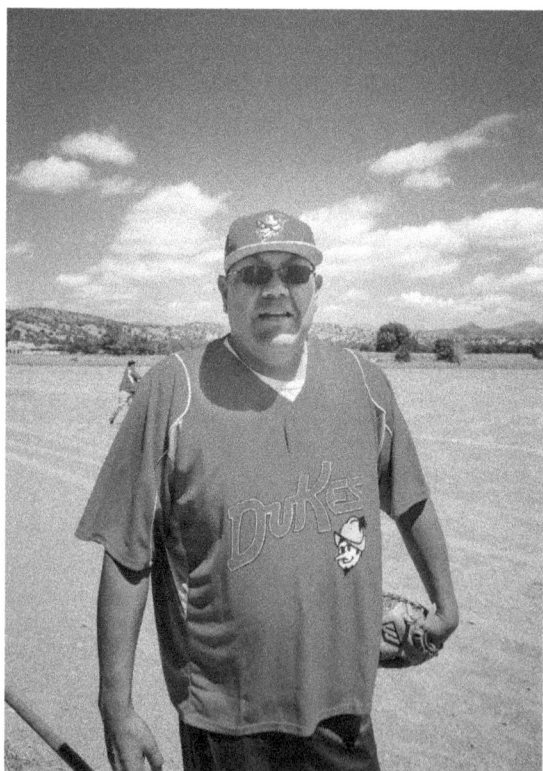

Towering Joel Aquero, son of Sam Aquero, has been a stalwart of Cochiti baseball since his early youth. His lifetime of stewardship under his father brought him to high levels of skill and leadership among his generation. Joel also excelled in basketball. He was a strong force while winning the state championship at Bernalillo High School. His forte was hitting home runs over the distant fences at the Cochiti field. He sometimes hit two or three home runs in a single game. Now, Joel is the coach and mentor to future generations. (Photograph by James Baker.)

Paul Herrera Jr. is part of a family of long-distance sluggers, like his father. Paul once hit a home run off the left-field scoreboard at Isotopes Park in a Pueblos/Navajos All-Star Game. Today, he maintains the family tradition, coaching his son, a left-handed catcher. Paul III, still in his early teens, plays adult baseball for the Dukes. (Photograph by James Baker.)

Here, three players from the Jemez Kyotes warm up. (Photograph by James Baker.)

NEW MEXICO'S PUEBLO BASEBALL LEAGUE

These children at a Dukes game have scrambled to get the best position on top of the dugout before a game starts. (Photograph by James Baker.)

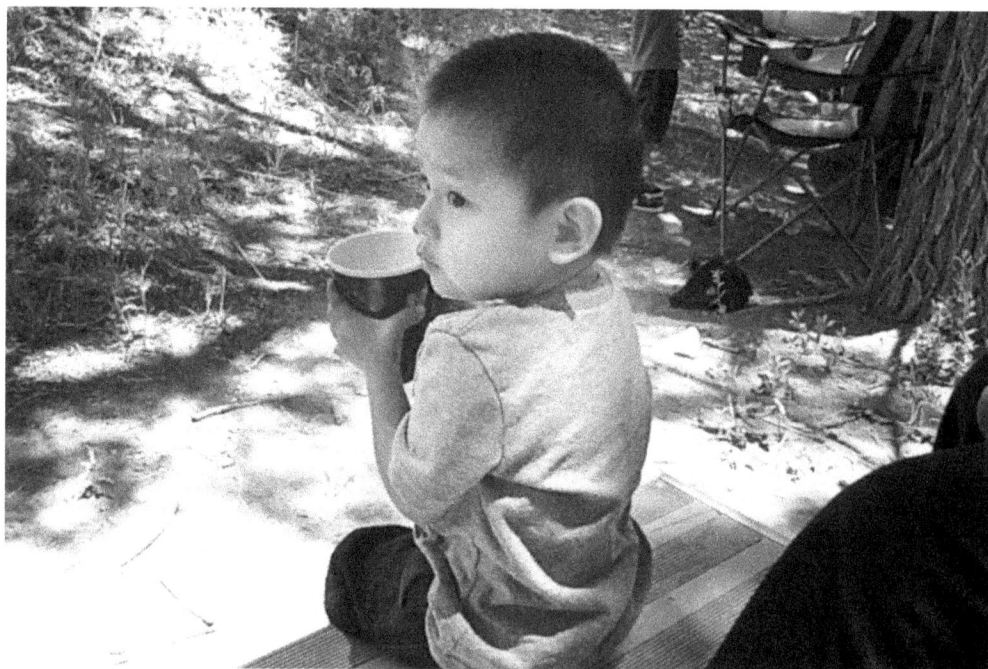

This two-year-old boy has a front-row seat at a Dukes game. He slurps his blue snow cone while remaining attentive to the game in front of him. He will later play with other children and local dogs, as well as talk to adults about using an iPad. This boy is an example of how young children grow up with the game and later emerge as players, coaches, longtime supporters, and maybe even umpires. (Photograph by Herb Howell.)

THE COCHITI BRAVES

The Braves and the Dukes are the current competing teams, but over the years there have been others. This is a Cochiti Brewers shirt. Other teams that have been mentioned are the Silversmiths, which preceded the Braves, and the Cochiti Rockies. (Photograph by James Baker.)

There has been considerable Pueblo history played on Braves Field. In photography, the idea of "a sense of place" denotes an area of rich human activity. There are people who believe that Braves Field is such a place. The final four photographs attempt to convey this feeling. This photograph shows part of the field from the bleachers. (Photograph by James Baker.)

THE COCHITI BRAVES

Shown here are the stands, located behind the backstop. (Photograph by James Baker.)

This is another "sense of place" photograph. It offers a view from inside the visitors' dugout. (Photograph by James Baker.)

THE COCHITI BRAVES

Shown here are home plate and the pitcher's mound. A ball has been left on the field, perhaps symbolic of the great game that will continue tomorrow and in the future in New Mexico's pueblos. (Photograph by James Baker.)

Visit us at
arcadiapublishing.com

· · · · · · · · · · · · · · · · · · · · · · · · · · · · · · · · · · · · · · · ·